TO BE SHARED

TO BE SHARED

Don't Waste the Gift that God Has Given You

Felice S.C

Right side publishing

This book is dedicated to the memory of my mother

(Miriam Kaye Alfred)

To the late Willie James Tillman Sr, and Bobbi Jean Tillman my Grandparents, also to the late Cora Billups my grandma

Contents

Acknowledgments viii
Introduction 1
He Who Holds the Future 2
Lord, Here I Am 3
Keep Going 4
Final Hour 6
Hanging 8
Wife 9
Depression 10
The Working Man 12
Poetry 13
Family 15
Beauty 17
Man 19
Saggars 21
Marriage 22
Success 24
Live 25
Happiness 26
Sister To Sister 27
God has a plan for me 29
Love From Above 31
Letter to Husbands 33
Don't Give Up 34
Master, Master 35
Make each Day Count 36
Gods' Time 37
My Children 38

How To Love	39
Close Encounters of the Divine Kind	40
He never said everything would be roses	41
Negativity	43
And These three Are one	45
Live for today	47
A Mothers Love	49
Let the world see Jesus in You	51
God's Beauty	53
Do you know Jesus	55
Empty Vessel	57
Flesh	58
"Seek Jesus First"	59
Why	60
The Mothers' Burden	62
Do you seek his face?	64
The Spice	65
He Holds Me Close	67
A Reason to Live	68
Cousins	69
Stop and Think	71
I Was A Slave	73
Anger	75
Stay On The Road	77
Indescribably Delicious	79
Women of glory prayer	80
Dad never said I love you!	81
A Precious Gift	82
He Cleared My Mind	83
God is immutable	84
One Way	85
My Bestfriend	87

A Spiritual Nurse	88
This life is exciting	90
Women Of God	91
Thy love and kindliness	92
No Rush	94
The Way To The Light	95
Life without you	96
Martin Luther King	97
Have faith	98
Never Alone	99
Complete	100
Silent pain	101
The Young and the Restless	103
Come Together	104
Micleicia Janell Tillman	106
John William Willis, Jr.	107
Johnesha Chante' Willis	108
Antalicia Kierah Gray	109
Try believing	110
I love You	111
Where's the church	112
A child born of a child	114
From a sister to a brother	116
My Life	118

Acknowledgments

I thank the Lord Jesus Christ, for giving me the gift of poetry to share with others. I thank my Pastor Bishop Lafayette Scales for encouraging all member of Rhema Christian Center to let the Lord lead and guide us. Thanks to Dan (Margret) Harris, for your prayer and encouragement. I thank my mother Miriam Kaye Alfred, she was my editor, inspire, and a poet herself. Look for her book soon to be published (The Way to the Light). Thanks to my dad, Ronald Burke. I thank my husband Robert Cauley for pushing me to finish my book, and loving me unconditionally. Thanks to my children, Micleicia, John, Johnesha, Antalicia, and my Godson Leonard for believing in me. I thank my family for encouraging me. Special thanks to my sister Kenyatta Alfred and my brother Christopher Weatherly, Aunts, Pasty Alston, Candace Tillman, Alvira Jones, Great aunt, Mary Pace. Uncles, Tyrea Tillman, Eric Tillman, Michael Alston, Great uncle Bishop Pace, for encouraging me. Special thanks to my cousins Monica Guidry (author of the book called Worship) and several other books, thank you Latonya (Wade) Crumwell, and Liza Mitchell, All of you are my cheerleaders, love you. To my little cousin Erica Tillman-Jefferson and my niece Jessica Weatherly keep writing, dreams do come true! Thanks to my sister, best friend Ebonie Banks, and my brother (John banks) you both have always been here for me.

Lots of love to my sister Mary Wayne, and my brother Ronald Burke, Thanks to my close friend Theresa Scott love you. Thanks to my mentors Bishop William Bibby of (New Covenant Church) Akron Ohio. God bless you and your wife as you continue to help others. Thank Linda Finch, (Phoebe Girls) Thanks to my mother n–love Joan Cauley. Thanks to my Godmother

Minister Barbara Thomas, and My God sisters Vivian Pitman, and Gwandine Thurmond, Thanks to my father n-love Robert barnes and his wife JoAnne Barnes, I love you both. Thanks to everyone who has listened to me read my poems, given me advice, prayed for me, and believed in me. There's too many of you to mention. I love you all.

Felice S.C

Introduction

To Be Shared

The gift of love, peace, hope, and encouragement with others through my life's experiences. I have realized my life is not my own. My mistakes and experiences are to be told. To show the power of God's grace and love. To help others overcome obstacles and challenges that we face in this life. My life is not my own. This world

Is not my home. The greatest gift is salvation through Jesus Christ. Through his blood, we receive the gift of eternal life. I pray that all who read this book will be blessed with peace, encouraged, find hope and seek

The kingdom of God first and all his righteousness. I pray that you are made whole and come to the realization that God's gifts are to be shared.

He Who Holds the Future

Oh, what a triangle our lives can be.

As we seek to find our future, which we cannot see.

Wondering in what direction we're headed,

and what path to take.

It sure would make things much easier,

if we would just trust our lives in the hands of,

(He Who Holds the Future)

My God, who has the master plan.

If we're on the path to destruction,

he'll make all corrections, to keep us from corruption.

No need for worry,

he has the master plan.

Don't get discouraged,

when you've lost your way,

He'll lead and guide you.

Lord, Here I Am

I need to touch you, draw close to you.

Hear your voice; you're what I need the most.

It's my choice to worship you, and you alone.

I long for your touch.

The rest I only feel when I'm in your arms, safe from all harm.

I know I've been at a distance for some time now.

No longer will I stand on the sidelines,

I'm moving in for a close encounter,

I'm ready to come to the dinner table and dine with you

Lord, here I am

Lord, here I am!

Feel my cup, let it overflow; I just want to grow in you.

Let me look like you, talk like you, walk like you, speak like you

Lord, here I am! Here I am!

To Be Shared

Keep Going

Imagine loving someone with everything in you,
yet there's nothing you can do to take away their pain.
Imagine, can you visualize a strong man,
as you watch, his strength begin to fail him?
This man, even though he's not well,
still laughs, and tells jokes too.
I remember my granddad's smile, soft and bright,
and his laugh, a deep chuckle,
just hearing that chuckle, made me laugh.
I remember his frown,
and the sternness in his voice.
And of course the fresh smell of his cologne.
I knew that granddad always knew someday he would go.

I know the strength he had will live on and live in me.
He spoke his mind; he left a lot of wisdom behind.
I've soaked that wisdom up with a sponge and will pass it on.
My Granddad used to always say,
"Girl whatever you do, don't just be in the world.
Live, have some pride in yourself.
If you mess up, don't stop, keep going."

As he did. He never stopped
He gave this life his best shot.
And when he messed up, he begged his pardon
(as he would say) but he kept going!
And we must keep going, we must keep going!
That's what Granddad would say to us now.

Final Hour

Life is full of uncertainties,

But one thing is for sure,

When our last hour has come,

There are no more deeds left to be done.

Nor words left to say.

All we need is love

We need not hear,

Judgments of what we should of or could have done.

When our last hour has come,

All we'll need is love.

All we'll need is love!

And Gods saving power.

We'll need kind words, lots of understanding.

Someone to hold our hand,

For one day our time will come,

And our life's journey will also come to an end.

We'll need rest and assurance for our soul.

Our loved one can't hear any words we may say now,

But in their final hour, they knew they were loved.

And of God saving power.

Felice S.C

In our final hour
In our final hour!
When that hour comes,
All we'll need is love
All we'll need is love!
And Gods saving power.
In our final hour,
We'll need Gods saving power.

Hanging

Sleepless nights, a restless heart,
Butterflies in the stomach,
Deep stairs into each other's eyes,
wondering minds.
Wanting to belong, not alone anymore
Scared, will this be heartbreak?
Or the beginning of a future.
Kisses that could go on, And on
Hugs that are so warm.
Letting go is not easy to do,
But it's hard not showing feeling,
Especially when holding back, makes you feel as if you're going to explode.
And if you explode there will be an overflow,
How much can you handle?
How much can you take?

Felice S.C

Wife

I knew who you were, even before you realized who you are.

I recognized the body from which my rib came from,

Even though the body seemed distraught on the outside,

I always knew what was inside.

And I always believed God would bring what was on the inside to the outside,

To complete me,

So I would forever abide in the body where I belong.

A body without a rib may function,

But a rib without a body cannot survive.

Until the body recognizes its own rib,

The rib is disconnected and cannot come home,

Unless the body reclaims it, as its own.

To Be Shared

Depression

Notice the word. De – means to stop.

Keyword, (press) to continue, moves forward or pushes.

When a person is de-press, they're down,

Usually, due to their situation.

When a person is in depression, they've fallen into a state of mind where they cannot see the brighter side of things.

If you look inside of the word

You can see the word press before the de came about in

Depression, Press existed.

When one began to look at the brighter side of things.

They began to change their state of mind.

That person can now press on.

We, as Christians should never be depressed.

For we know with God all things are possible.

There's always hope. How can we be depressed and yet say we have faith in God.

In God, there's no room for (de) or (press ion)

Only pressing on, moving forward in his will. We must not put the (de) in press. The (de) belongs to the devil. Who is defeated? Defeat!

Stopped in his tracks. Power belongs to God. There is nothing too hard for God.

Nothing!

The Working Man

He woke up and fell,
On his knees to pray.
Thank you, Lord, for my family.
After praying, he kissed his wife,
Fixed breakfast then drove his daughter to the bus stop.
When he arrived at work, he greeted his co-workers,
Sat down at his desk, and thanked God again quietly.
Throughout the day,
he gave much advice, encouragement, and smiles.

Works not always easy,
Life is full of challenges,
There's always a decision to make.
Things to do, not enough hours in a day.
Men, remember your day will be full,
But make time for family.
The love of God will carry you to your destination,
Your hard work will pay off, In Jesus name

Poetry

Writing to me is simple, not complicated! It is my best!

My thoughts and feelings put on paper.

Others live I have seen,

my ink pen is no mystery

Let it not be to you

It's what I think what I believe

What others will see on paper

yet not know my inner thoughts

Writings a gift that comes from within my soul,

when I let go

that's when the words began to flow,

It is then……It's then that I am free.

Free to give of me what's hidden within
Writing to me is simple, not complicated!
It's my best that is heard by many
wisdom to live on………and on
Guidance forever strong
More than a pen can deliver, but a message
That paper can carry.
IT IS MY BEST!

Family

There are many up's and downs in the family.
No one's family is perfect.

We cannot change the family that God has given us.
Complaining will not get us anywhere.

I often ask the question, is blood thicker than water?

Will the water run out or will the blood dry up?

Family is all about relationships.

Some through the bloodline, some through the water baptism of Jesus Christ.

We can't change our bloodline, but we can embrace what God has given us.

That's where our strength lies.

That where hope is.

It's the friend, that's closer than a sister.

The neighbor that's more like family,

Maybe the cousin that always seems to take the words right out of our mouth.

The uncle that's like a father

Whoever we have true relationships with is our family, through blood or the water baptism of Jesus Christ.

Blood or water, I need Both, I'll take both.

Beauty

Beauty is rosy cheeks,

greasy lips and big eyes

a lightweight gut,

and a booty

that shakes

from side to side.

Beauty is

collard greens between her teeth

and the smell of Chanel number 5 on her neck,

Beauty is not what you see when you look in the mirror,

but it's hidden inside

Beauty is not around the corner,

Not on the block!

but at your doorsteps

knocking, knocking

You don't hear her.

Beauty is

you know her!

You talk to her every day.

Man

A man carries the weight and forms the path of the next generation.

No matter what the load may be, He carries it to the destiny of the future Generation,

through guidance, teaching, leadership, and education.

Reaching out to young men and boys, carrying the burden of this wife and daughters.

A strong shoulder to lean and depend on,

A firm hand for correction by direction,

Words of knowledge and encouragement

through strength, character, love, and patience.

To Be Shared

By Example

Understanding that he may make mistakes, but as long as he has breath, he is not a failure.

A man acknowledges what he has behind him and accepts the challenges ahead.

He does what he is lead to do to make sure his family is fed, in the right way

He may stumble, he may fall, but he always survives

He's the protector of many lives.

Saggars

How can they say we are a waste
going down the wrong path?
Is it because we let our pants sag,
and have tattoos and grills?
Could it be our Afros and love for music?
Someone said it's the way we look and speak,
our neighborhoods and surroundings.
Why do these people always ask about our mothers?
Today, I will pull up my pants,
Speak well.

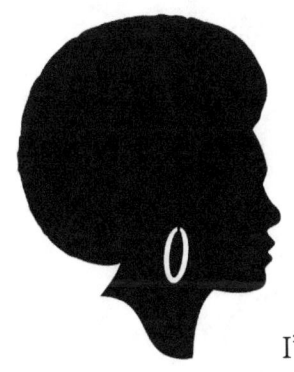

I'm creating the image I want the world to see.
Now, my Afro is mine.
My Afro, My Afro
I have no desire to change.

Marriage

The air is not always clean,

Sometimes it's full of dust and debris.

We breathe it together.

Yesterday we climbed a mountain

today we're in a valley.

Tomorrow is yet to come,

we face the unknown together.

Your dreams are not mines,

I'll help you fulfill them.

I don't agree with you on all things,

I'll try to understand by learning your language.

We will put our hope in Jesus.
I'll follow you as you follow Christ.
When you're wrong, I'll go to the Father,
he will help me concentrate on my flaws,
while he fixes yours.
When faced with a decision,
We'll go to the father together.
Together we'll go to the Father!
Together we'll go to the Father!

To Be Shared

Success

When your feet touched the floor,

the doors to success swung open.

Follow the plan,

your destiny awaits.

Keep walking!

Keep walking!

Keep walking!

Remember to walk through the doors

Live

I think I'll go sky diving,
why not
What am I afraid of?
It is God who determines when I will die.
I can only determine how I live my life.
I'm glad he gave me that choice,
because I could never choose a day to die.
Or how about scuba diving,
What are you afraid of?
Don't let the enemy cripple you with fear.
Christ died for us.
So, we must live for him!

Happiness

Is peace within,
that shows throughout our lives.
Happiness,
Is a resting soul with a pure heart,
abiding in God, safe, and secure.
Happiness,
Is not fearing what's ahead,
because of the peace in God's word and what he said.
It's abiding in hope, love, and resting in the master's arms.

To be happy, we must release all the pain,
and take hold and proclaim,
the royalties and righteousness of God.
True happiness,
Is when the smile we have on the inside
can overshadow our frown,
leaving them never to be found.

Sister To Sister

If I can just reach out to you now
to laugh, cry, listen, talk, and walk together.
Anything I can do for you today,
to let you know, I am here.
You must not suffer alone,
tomorrow might be too late.
I must say, I love you today.
You are my sister
You have all the beauty that God had left,
after making me
You're indeed beautiful!
I see all my strength and love in you.
Everything you do keeps me going.
Without you, there's no me.

God has a plan for me

My plans always seem to fail.
But God has a plan for me!
He turns my failures into success.
When my strength fails and I can no longer fight,
he holds me tight.
I'm climbing a mountain that continues to go down.
I turn to the left then to the right,
round and round in circles,
back to the beginning is where I always end up.
(Never Winning)
God has a plan for me!
I cry daily and try to fulfill my destiny.
Searching for answers that there are no questions to.

All things work together for the good
of those that love the Lord.
So, what is God's plan for me?
God has a plan for me!
As sure as I exist
He insist that he has a plan for me,
I see my reflection in the mirror,
Yet I'm no closer to me than God is to me.
I am accountable for what I do,
But God is in control of who I am,
he controls my destiny.
God does have a plan for me.

Love From Above

When I close my eyes, I think and wonder,

why does he love me so much?

Even when I'm wrong, he holds me ever so close,

he loves me most.

I don't deserve this type of love at all.

As stubborn as I am,

he keeps on doing great things for me.

I don't listen sometimes, yet he still speaks to me.

And when I'm down on my knees with no words to say,

he still hears me.

I've drifted so far away from him,

yet he still sees me and reaches down

with his mighty hand and retrieves me.

When I close my eyes, I can hear his voice softly saying,

I love you. You are my child.

I don't deserve this type of love.

I know even if I were perfect,

I'd still be undeserving of his love.

Letter to Husbands

There are times that we don't make
you feel as amazing as you make us feel.
The message that we want to relay to you
is loud in our ears, but you don't hear the horns blowing.
We'd like to tell you that when you walk into a room,
we hear bells ringing.
We see the sun shining, rainbows in the sky.
We may argue, but our love for you never dies
Please see us just as you did on our wedding day.
Know that love is not easy,
marriage is a commitment worth the work.
What God puts together, we will not put asunder.
We can be our own worst enemy,
Let us not self-destruct.

Don't Give Up

Sometimes the road on which we travel is long and hard,

going for miles and miles,

seeming not to get very far.

Stop, if you may along the way.

Take a rest break, but don't give up.

Tears may fill your eyes; the pain will come.

The main thing is to stay focused

Many others have been down the same road as you,

and have now made it.

Don't give up!

Master, Master

In your hands, we give our lives,

for you have the master plan.

You understand our ups and downs.

When we're crying out, no one's around,

to you, we bow.

Oh, lord

Oh, lord

hear us now,

we need thee near, to lead and guide us.

Jesus, Jesus

When the roads are dark, you know the way.

Help us now, we pray.

Give us the grace to finish this here race.

Make each Day Count

If you could walk a mile in my shoes,
maybe see my pain for one day,
then you would understand.
I guess I can live my life the best way I can,
But the more I try, the harder each day gets.
Life is short, I've learned a lot.
Everything I've been through,
I can't go back and give myself
the strength to fill in what I lacked.
But through all my pain,

If I've helped someone, made someone laugh
That's the main thing. If
I've shared something to make someone else strong.
That's what counts.
And maybe I wasn't all wrong,
Perhaps I've done something right!
It sure would make all the pain that I have experienced
in this life, worth it.
For in the next life I shall wear a crown.

Felice S.C

Gods' Time

The lord only knows why he has allowed

you to endure so much pain these last years.

Just know your love one suffers no longer.

There's nothing you've done wrong.

As you may ask the question of why me?

It's just Gods' time.

And in time, you and your loved ones will meet again.

Until then,

try and remember all the reasons

why you loved them so.

Let those reasons help you to go on.

Know that you have friends and family who love you here.

We're your strength when you're weak.

Lean on them.

With Gods' help,

in time you'll make it through.

My Children

God loves me so much that he has shared such a special gift with me

Not one, or, two, it's greater than three, He's given me four children.

Four to love and hold. What a blessing bestowed.

Though he has given me time

to spend with them, these children are not mine.

Micleicia, John, Johnesha, and Antalicia

They're God's children. He has lent them to me,

He let me borrow them, to have and to hold, to love and help them grow.

Oh, he loves me so much.

We laugh, talk, play, whatever the day brings,

great or small, we face it together.

God places these four children with me! For how long, I don't know

Such a great gift he has bestowed.

My love for them I will forever show

God has placed these four with me it's hard watching them

grow into young women and men

It's not easy watching them make mistakes.

I wish I could protect them from every bump and heartache.

God gave them to me, and I gave each one back to him

Felice S.C

How To Love

The way I love you is how I want to be loved.

What I share with you,

I love for you to share the same.

A smile given should be a smile returned.

A kind word said, should be heard.

A warm thought should be shared.

Touch doesn't always mean one cares.

Hugs aren't hugs unless they're given,

It sure would make one feel the warmth of love.

Time spent together should be well valued.

Take time out of a busy day for some quality time.

Learn how to love now.

Days passed are not returned.

Close Encounters of the Divine Kind

I was down on my knees praying one day,
when I first met this man named Jesus.
It was a close encounter of the Devine Kind-
one I had never experienced before.
It seemed to engulf my whole being
as I knelt there on the floor.
This bright light traveling towards me
as never, ever before.
It was hard to snap back to earth-
I was feeling so good, like I was in Heaven.
I had truly had a close encounter of the Divine Kind.

Ms.Miriam K. Alfred

He never said everything would be roses

God never promised us a rose garden.

He never said everything would be sweet,

or even go our way.

What he did promise,

he'd be there each day. Every step of the way

to smell the roses.

When every thing's going right,

and when things aren't so sweet.

My God will take that bitter taste away.

God never said there wouldn't be any pain.

Nor did he say life on this earth would last forever.

But he did say if we strive with him awhile,

he'll give us eternal life.

He said weeping may endure for a night,

but joy cometh in the morning.

This too will pass.

Nothing stays the same,

everything must change.

God never said the road in which we travel would be smooth.

He promised to walk with us,

even until the end.

To Be Shared

He never said life would be fair.

He did say,

he would create a new heaven and earth,

separate the good from the b

He promised to renew our strength if we wait on him.

I 'm glad God is the same yesterday as he is today.

He's the only one

that will never change.

Negativity

People will always have something to say.

Some things will build, restore, give hope, encourage, and enlighten.

Negativity destroys, tares down, never offers hope, peace, or encouragement.

Negativity drains; it will drain the life out of you.

Positivity will add and bring life to you.

Add

Subtract

Subtract negative people from your life.

Don't let them speak a word over your life.

Stop them in their tracks!

Do not let the words they speak manifest in your life.

Add positive people to your life who will help build and restore you.

Leave no room for

NEGATIVITY!

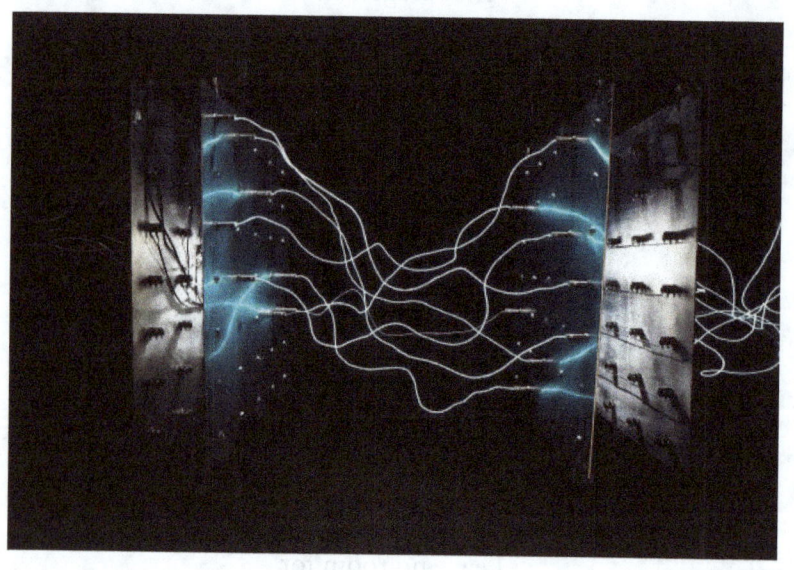

And These three Are one

The father – God,
who has given us life,
He created us from dust,
which we'll all return.
The son- Jesus Christ,
the father manifest in the flesh,
to show us how to live each day.
Yet he the father gave his son,
that we might have a right to the tree of life.

The ultimate sacrifice!

The Holy Spirit –

sent to us through his son the Lord Jesus Christ.

Left behind as a comforter, to lead and guide us to all truth.

A spiritual communicator to the father.

And these three

are one!

Live for today

Worry not what tomorrow may bring,

or what yesterday has brought.

Yesterday is gone. Tomorrow is yet to be seen.

Oh, such a load to carry,

as we worry from day today.

When we think about tomorrow,

which we may not see,

today is passing us by.

Passing us by fast!

Enjoy today while it lasts.

If we're blessed to see tomorrow,

we'll only wish we didn't let yesterday pass us by so fast. So much to do today.

Tomorrow will take care of its self.

Just as God takes care of us.

Felice S.C

A Mothers Love

Her love will find you at your lowest point and encourage you when you feel as if you can't go on.

Her love stretches and reaches out to you,

No matter what you do, you can't replace her love

Nothing can fill her space.

She's always there to see you through, whatever you must face.

She guides you through life's journey.

Although you make mistakes and do wrong, her love remains forever strong.

No one can replace a mother's love. No One

She'll stay up all night crying and praying for her children; asking the Lord to keep them safe.

She'll sacrifice all she has, even go without

Just as long as her children are provided for. That's all she cares about.

NO ONE CAN REPLACE A MOTHER'S LOVE.

NO ONE!

My mother, Miriam Kaye Alfred, gave so much: her smile, giving heart, words of wisdom, and the gift of poetry. I hope that others will always remember her and that her legacy will live on.

MOTHER & CHILD

Let the world see Jesus in You

When you walk, take Christ along

When you hope, hope in Jesus

When you speak, speak words of life

Speak the truth, what is right

When you touch someone,

touch them with the life of Christ.

I in him, and he in me.

For the world to see!

When you show the world something,

Show them the way,

as Christ has shown you the way.

Let them know

Jesus Christ.

Let them know

Jesus Christ!

Felice S.C

God's Beauty

Sunshine, flowers, sweet smells in the air

Valleys and valleys of Lilies

Rivers and rivers that flow forever deep

Honey on a vine candlelight with wine

Rainbows across the sky

Stars so bright, grass so green, trees so clean,

wind so smooth and soothing.

(This is Gods beauty)

Birds chirping

Lightning across the sky

Thunder that roars

Makes one wonder and marvel how

God could create such beauty.
With his voice, he created everything of choice.
Such power without hands,
he designated a master plan.
Children laughing and playing,
Oh what a treasure, there's no measure.
For this is the beauty of God!

Felice S.C

Do you know Jesus

Do you know him?

Have you tried to find him?

Are you looking around for a man?

Have you got peace in your heart?

A love ever lasting

Faith that overshadows, visions hard to see.

Hope and reassurance, of eternal life.

Do you know Christ?

Have you asked him to forgive you?

Say lord come into my heart

I no longer want to be a sinner,

I want you as my Lord and savior Jesus Christ.

I can't make it on my own.

Did you once know him?

Have you left home?

He wants to know you

To show you his love

He's not hard to find

clear your mind

Say lord,

I come to you today,

forgive me, lord,

come into my heart

save me.

Take control of my life,

make me whole.

I want to live right,

I want to know Christ.

Say that prayer,

and you will know Jesus Christ,

Your life will never be the same!

Empty Vessel

I will not be an empty vessel,
just collecting dust!
No, I will live my life to the fullest for
Jesus Christ!
Each day of my life I will rise in the
name of Jesus!
Ready to serve, reaching out
to teach others,
and share with others what God
has given to me.
I will not be an empty vessel,
Collecting dust!
No longer will I remain on the self
I'm pouring the contents of my vessel out.
To nourish the earth.
As I pour into others life
God will continue to fill my vessel

Flesh

I'm in a struggle. It's a wrestling heart and soul.
It's a wresting heart and soul.
I'm trusting and believing in God.
His promise, I won't let go of.
This struggle I know was won,
when Jesus flesh was crucified on the cross,
for all who were, and are lost.
I'm in a struggle it's not with my heart or my soul,
That's a lie that I've been told.
The struggle,
Is with my F L E S H!

My heart I gave to God, my soul is his.
My flesh I must crucify daily, and not let it rise.
I must never forget that Christ died for me.
He forgave my sins,
now I must confess my sins, daily
change my ways and never forget,
never forget that he died for me!

"Seek Jesus First"

In every little thing you do
you should learn to seek Jesus first!
Whether it be a job, career, school, or marriage
seek him first, because he'll never lead you wrong.
He'll always give you the best advice
because he's the greatest counselor, you could ever have.
So throughout your daily routine in life
learn to always seek Jesus first
He'll never steer you wrong.

Ms. Miriam K. Alfred

Why

Are you angry?

Are you angry?

Are you hurting?

Are you hurting?

Why?

Are you sad?

Are you sad?

Why?

Did someone make you angry?

Did someone hurt you?

Did they make you sad?

Can someone make you be or feel, anyway they want to?

Do you believe that we all have a choice in all situations?

Then why be angry?

It gets the heart pumping pretty fast.

You won't last too long, carring anger.

Why keep on hurting?

Let God heal your heart

Don't keep feeling the pain……

The Mothers' Burden

Take up the Mothers' Burden

All the work and nine months of pain;

just so our life can maintain.

Fathers leaving, thinking it's a game.

Take up the Mother's Burden

When she tries to hide the truth

Even though he leaves her with bruises,

She will always tell you she can make it through.

Take up the Mothers' Burden

Knowing she can't get away and her life is another song that's been played.

Take up the Mothers' Burden

Let's scream and shout,

and show the world what mothers are about,

and let everyone know you can't live without.

Take up the Mothers' Burden

Quit making the mother's look wrong

They work two jobs, and still standing strong.

Take up the Mothers' Burden

When she is alone, living in a small apartment and feels like it's not a home.

Three kids, making it on her own

Take up the Mothers' Burden

All the time when she feels stress, thinking her life is a mess

No one is telling her that she is doing her best.

Take up the Mothers' Burden

Overcome the bad things in life.

And after these things happen, she is still willing to fight,

Knowing that she can go to sleep at night,

The weight on her shoulder is now light.

Take up the Mothers' Burden. MS. Johnesha Willis

Do you seek his face?

Today when you rose,

Did you fall down on your knees?

Did you thank him?

Did you seek his face, and ask for direction?

Or have you just chosen to go on through the day,

as if you just rose.

Did you ask the Lord Jesus Christ?

The one who knows all,

to lead and guide you today.

How can you go on your way without even stopping to say thank you,

to the one who has given you your life.

Is it right to ask for help when you're struggling throughout the day? But, not seeking his face in the morning?

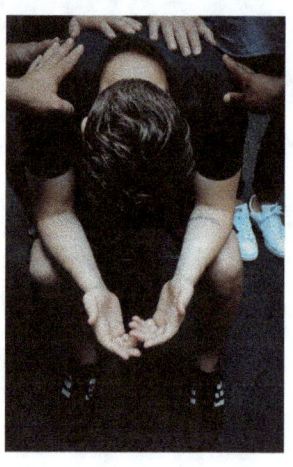

The Spice

Time goes slow when you don't even know a loved one,

but, when they're gone, time goes fast.

As you take your last look upon your father's body,

You may feel as if you've been alone without him all your life,

but God has given you the spice that was missing in his life.

This world isn't fair,

Only God can fill the emptiness that maybe there

He's been your father from day one.

To Be Shared

He's loved you ever so much,

and will carry you through whatever rough roads that may be ahead.

Hold on to the spice

Put it in your life

Hold on to the spice

Hold on to the spice

Stand for what is right

Hold on to the spice.

He Holds Me Close

The love of Jesus has touched me so dear,

When others weren't around

He held me near.

Though times I was lonely and fell astray,

I knew that in Jesus' arms, I had to stay.

Ms. Miriam K. Alfred

A Reason to Live

If you just exist from day-to-day,

And it seems as though you're sleeping your life away,

Just give it up to Jesus

He'll turn it around,

He'll place your feet on solid ground.

He'll give you a joy you've never known before,

You won't be able to wait for each new morning!

Yes,

He'll give you a reason to live,

and you'll be so excited to see,

what he will do each new day that you rise.

Yes, He'll give you a reason to live!!!

Ms. Miriam K. Alfred

Cousins

Cousins keep the next
Generation going,
when sisters and brothers are arguing,
cousins stick together,
They weather the storms and chase rainbows.
Sing songs, cry many tears, share stories, laughs, and jokes.
No matter what they keep the yoke between them strong.

They keep the generation going.
They reach beyond the walls of their lives to help others.
Cousins have abound that can't be explained, only maintain

Stop and Think

When it rains, do you know the sun will come out
after a while?
When the sun shines, know one day it will rain!
When you're right, just know one day you'll be wrong.
Your cabinets may be full now,
Don't you know that one day it may be empty!
Today you'll learn a lesson,
Tomorrow you may teach a lesson.
Have you ever looked at the drunkard on the street?
Can't you see beyond his drunkard state?
One day he may be sober
Do you see the drunkard?
Because you were once drunk?
Don't look so hard!
What about the children?
Were you once a child?

Are you married?

Remember,

You were once single.

Were you once hopeless?

you now have hope.

Turn the other cheek!

Did you hit someone once?

Were you ever broke?

Now you have money……

Now you have money……

Do you know for sure that you'll N E V E R……. be BROKE?

I Was A Slave

Laugh, smile, and rejoice,

I am free!

I was filthy, scared, my heart Shattered and torn into pieces.

I never knew that a human being Could treat another human so cruel!

I worked day and night, night and day picking cotton, and working the fields.

My baby was stolen, taken from me!

They took my child from me!

I dare not say he is my masters' child!

Master, Master, please

ONE, TWO, THREE, FOUR, FIVE, SIX!

I can't count how many times they hit me!

Laugh, smile, and rejoice.

I'm free now!

Whether by death or release, don't worry about me

I'm in the master's hands, I'll always remember what happens to me,

I see the scares. Yet I forgive.

I'm free, I'm free!

Laugh, smile, and rejoice

I'm free now!

Felice S.C

Anger

My heart is racing its beating fast. I'd like to get my hands

On him or her, if I could!

I don't know why, when, or even how I became angry.

I just am!

My muscles are tense, I can hardly breathe. I feel like there's no relief.

I don't know why, when or even how long I've been this way.

I just am.

No hope, no faith, no tears, no more smiles,

just frowns!

I like to get my hands on him or her, maybe punch a hole

In a wall!

Some people are angry for no reason.

They are just mad at the world. I think they've

Been mad for so long,

that they don't even know why!

To be angry for a long time is like an infirmity.

Anger can cause heart problems, disease, and

all kinds of sickness.

Make a choice,
Stop being angry.
Learn how to smile.
Reach for hope, you'll gain faith.
Through your faith
you'll find God and peace of mind!

Stay On The Road

Stop when it's time to stop.

Follow the lights.

Move forward, move forward.

Change lanes if you must,

But stay on the road.

If you get lost,

follow the signs.

The word of God.

Don't go too far over the lines,

This road is straight and narrow.

With guidelines to follow.

Sometimes the road is dark and long.

You may feel like the only one on the road.

Just keep moving, don't let others distract you.

You're responsible for the vehicle that you're traveling in.

Your body is the temple of the lord.

You may need a tune-up!

Give God some praise.

Practice now,

Because there is an end to this road.

It's called heaven.

Oh, and there's a party going on.

STAY ON THE ROAD!

Indescribably Delicious

As they say about the mound bar;

I have found this true of Jesus.

He is indescribably delicious.

The more you get to know him, the sweeter he is.

Oh, how we need to taste and see that the Lord is good!

Miriam Kaye Alfred

Women of glory prayer

Our prayer is Lord Restore us back to our original design, so we can walk out the plan that you have for our lives: as Daughters, Mothers, Sisters, Wives, Teachers, Pastors, Evangelist, Ministers, whatever you want us to be. Lord, we want to represent your glory, your holy presence. We ask you to use us to help restore the broken shaken and empty. We're believing in your saving power, grace, mercy, love, eternal peace in this life, and the life to come. We know that you are not just our savor, but our father! Lord, we trusted and depend on you in every area of our lives. Lord, we want to shine for you! Lord, we want your Presents to lead and guide us, so your glory will be seen in us. We honor, love and adore you. Thank you, Lord! Thank you, Jesus!

Dad never said I love you!

Letter from your father (Jesus)

I am here when you need someone to talk to.

Someone to say good job, son. You may have never

Heard those words from your natural father. Listen close,

Good job, son, I love you most! I've seen your hard work.

I've heard your silent tears. I know your fear, even

Before you do. You've passed the test, and pushed

Through the mess. Your father, you loved unconditional. I

love you unconditional, unconditional.

My son, it's not easy to love someone when they act like

They don't even care about you. Oh, my son, remember

when you didn't even know me as your

Father? I still loved you. I chasten after you. I forgave

You when you went against my word. Oh, my son, I

know it hurts to love your father, and not feel the love in

Return. I want you to think of the cross that I bear for

your sins, what a price to pay! I know you didn't

deserve my love: The father I

gave you here on earth didn't either, but you loved him

unconditional like I love you.

To Be Shared

A Precious Gift

I thought I'd never meet a man who had a heart like mine. Who could see things as I see them. A man who has the desire to touch peoples' lives, such as I do. Meeting you is like putting the pieces together to a puzzle. The little things in you, I see, which are significant to me. Like your smile, words of truth, and a pure heart. A man who bears good fruit, a love that's strong, and does no wrong. All that I see in you, others may have known:

Yet missed!

I'm glad you have chosen to share the precious gift of you with me.

He Cleared My Mind

My mind was all a clutter;

Didn't know what to do,

Or just what direction in life to take.

Then, I called on Jesus, and he gave me a reason to pray.

Now, He leads and guides me each and every step of the way.

I found everything that I needed in him.

He gave me perfect peace.

And he'll do the same for you- just trust him and you will

See!

Ms. Miriam K Alfred

To Be Shared

God is immutable

In this world, there are so many uncertainties,

But one thing is for sure,

the love of God will never change no matter how imperfect we are.

Dear Lord,

In my darkest hour is when I long for you the most.

When I don't deserve your love is when I need you the most.

In my despair, you're always there.

Even though I'm so undeserving of your love,

You have never cast me away.

Time after time, I mess up, yet you still bless me.

One Way

You thought you could get around going through the door.

So, you tried to climb through a window,

unaware that the door was unlocked.

All you had to do was open it.

So afraid that someone would see you

if you walked down the aisle and gave your heart to God,

He holds the key.

He's the door!

Your sins, you thought you were hiding them.

You can't sneak in through a window or back door.

God sees all.

The pastor, teacher, minister, deacons, and evangelist all came through the door.

The way of the cross. (Jesus Christ)

We all were lost, just like you.

You try and cover your shame with clothing,

yet, you're still naked before the Lord.

He is the only way: the truth and the light.

No one compares to him. No one!

My Bestfriend

I search half my life looking for a true friend.

Then one day a little voice spoke to me and said,

I'll be the best friend you ever had.

I won't turn my back on you

when the going gets tough,

you can lean on me and trust in me for the rest of your life.

Yes, I found a friend in Jesus,

and He's the best friend I've ever had.

He gives me sweet melodies

to sing that ring deep down in my soul.

He put my life back in order and took full control.

I'm so glad to call him my best friend!

Miriam Kaye Alfred

A Spiritual Nurse

Many come to work, and they're just a body that's there.
When this nurse works, she really cares.
She has a lot to share.
When she goes down the hall, there are smiles everywhere.
It might look like she's just passing meds,
to the unbeliever who's misled
This nurse fulfills the need to be fed by
spreading the word of God daily.
Now if you're a believer, you'll notice her bright smile.
You'll see how she represents Christ.

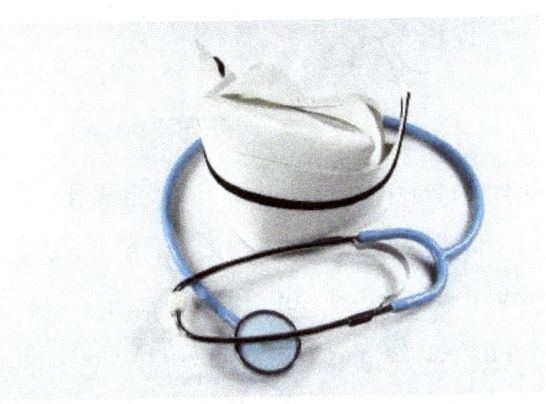

Sometimes you may even hear a low melody coming from her lips.

As she gives God the glory and silently prays for each patient.

Sorry if she offends you, nonbelievers,

But we as believers need this type of nurse.

I say keep singing, keep on praising, and if I ever come your way,

say a silent prayer for me too………

To Be Shared

This life is exciting

I'm excited to wake up each morning with a man of God. Someone that loves and adores me. I don't have to wonder Where my life is headed, but I know in what direction I'm Headed. I'll create a plan in the will of the lord, and watch Things manifest in my life. Life in God is so exciting!

It doesn't mean that I'm perfect,

Just that I know the perfect One.

We are cool; he guides me and corrects me.

Life in Jesus is exciting!

Women Of God

You have the right to remain silent (keep your mouth shut!)

Anything you say will be heard by your father, and he is your judge.

You have a right to an attorney. (Your father)
He will defend you.

He is your advocate; the Holy Spirit is your guide.

You have the right to plead your case before the judge in prayer

As your father examines you, you will be given time to change your ways and not your husbands.

His father will deal with him.

You are ordered to forgive and encourage your husband.

The husband has the right to lead his family by the order of God.

He will plead his family's case before the Lord,

and ask for help when he doesn't understand.

He will let his wife be his helpmate.

The Holy Spirit will be their guide.

To Be Shared

Thy love and kindliness

I am dirty Lord.
I seek to be pure.
I've been dirty before.
You have cleansed me.
My sins to see no more
Father I'm ashamed,
for the sins, I commit
is yet the same.
I've asked for forgiveness
Thou have forgiven me
Thou love and kindness,
you have bestowed.

If I fall yet shall you, raise me up again

Thou love and kindness,

Mercy everlasting

Thy hand that grabs me in,

to mend my crooked ways.

Thy love and kindness cover a multitude.

Of sin!

No Rush

Running but not getting anywhere.

Walking seems to get me there faster than when I run.

When I walk I notice the flowers, the trees, birds,

and all that nature has to offer.

I don't think that I have accomplished all that I have to achieve in this life.

So, I've been in a rush to get things done.

When I'm rushing, I miss a lot of essential details.

I'm slowing the pace.

Slowing my pace,

Staying focused and moving forward.

Wow!

Now I can hear instructions from the Lord.

Sometimes he'll say move fast, slow down, or wait,

And even not yet.

I can hear him say no,

because I'm not running.

When I do run, I run to Him. Then I slow

down and let him lead.

There's no need to rush as long as

I let him lead

I will accomplish all that he needs me to achieve in this life

The Way To The Light

The Way to the Light is simple than we think.

Though it may get dark sometimes,

It won't always stay that way.

Remember- the darkest moment is just before the breaking of day.

So, if you're traveling in a tunnel of darkness,

just reach out to Jesus.

He will lead you to

the Way to The Light!!!!

By Miriam K Alfred

Life without you

Life without you,

well, it was very empty.

There was a big hole in my heart.

Oh! How I tried to fill that hole, in and out of relationships.

Lonely,

Wondering why.

I built my own wall of protection and sealed my heart, so no one could touch it.

My life was a struggle.

I would get tired of being alone, so I'd give someone a try.

More heartaches. Now I have you:

If I would have just waited On God, He gave me the best he had to give!

Martin Luther King

A young black man who had a dream.

That dream brought many to freedom.

They say the way he died was odd and sad.

People were mad.

Now he's gone to a kingdom above.

His love he left behind.

People were still put in a bind.

You say you don't understand, someone great fought for freedom.

The cost was high.

His life he lost!

What we lack is Martin.

What we can't bring back is him.

What he gave, saved blacks, whites, yellow, red, and brown.

He stood up for all people.

He brought us this far,

we must let freedom ring through sorrow and all tomorrows.

Have faith

You say your day will never come.

I say it will!

It will!

Your day will come. All your hard work will pay off soon!

Tired of struggling, wondering, and worrying.

The some Ole, some Ole daily routine.

Just when you thought things would get better,

It gets worse!

You don't know what else to do but cry.

You'll get through it somehow.

The pain only lasts for a while.

I say your day will come, you say that's easy for me to say…

It will be okay! Have faith, this too shall pass

Never Alone

You may feel lonely- much of the time,

Though you're always surrounded by crowds.

But this you must know,

You are never truly alone-

Not if Jesus lives in your heart.

He will walk with you, and talk with you-

Even in your darkest hour.

If you'll just take the time to listen,

then you will hear His still, small voice, and know that you are never alone,

no never alone.

By Miriam K. Alfred

Complete

You have touched my heart.
You've made me feel whole and complete.
With you by my side, I am totally unique.
Our love will blossom.
We'll reach higher heights, with our dreams in sight.
Believing in each other will relieve our stress.
We are diffidently at our best together
We can conquer all!

Silent pain

Wake up in the morning, It's a new day.

Not much has changed.

God has blessed you to see this day,

you must be grateful, and try to get through it somehow.

It's so strange to think that this day would be

any different than the rest.

How could it be so hard to get through one day?

Having to remind yourself to eat.

Having to encourage yourself to get up.

As if you have something to look forward to.

Everyone feels like your lazy, or you must be crazy.

(SILENT PAIN)

Tired of T.V. Tired of the same Ole same Ole.

Trying to find love in yourself.

Maybe that helped you get through the day.

So you think that someone else will give you love.

They don't understand.

You know the saying if you don't love yourself, who will?

You toss and turn at night, you can't sleep.

Wondering will tomorrow be fun, or will someone see your pain.

Looking for a smile, Maybe a hug.

You try to do what's right, yet things turn out wrong.

(SILENT PAIN)

There's help if you're suffering in silence.

I Say to you God loves us even when we don't love our self.

Every day we face challenges.

We must trust in God, God alone. Not ourselves.

If you're feeling this way, you're in a deep depression

Give your life to God!

Each morning you get up, say thank you (Jesus).

Ask for his guidance.

You must make yourself eat. I say to you get out of bed.

Stop listening to the devils lies.

Speak positive words over your own life.

Don't wait for anyone to bring you hope. Reach for hope, grab it. Hope in Jesus!

Study Gods word, the King James Version or NIV

No more silent pain.

Today is a new day for you, my friend. In Jesus name

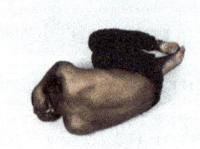

The Young and the Restless

We all go through life searching-
For what, we do not know.
Through drugs, alcohol, and such,
But all these things don't bring about
Much.
The joy, the peace that we are looking
For- is knocking, knocking at our hearts
Door.
If only we would answer, we would find
What we have spent a lifetime searching
For.
Jesus is his name!

Miriam K Alfred

Come Together

Will you,

Will you,

Please give up that religious facade?

Want you,

Want you quit looking at others, and look at yourself?

Can we,

Can we, of different ministries come together in the name of Jesus Christ?

If we would not see Apostolic, Baptist, Catholic, etc.

But all come together as one,

confessing the name of Jesus Christ,

How many are we losing,

because we as believers waste our time evangelizing one another?

And not reaching out to the lost.

We may disagree on a lot of things,

Can we,

Can we agree on Christ?

Christ Jesus as our savior.

Micleicia Janell Tillman

I am the soul of my ancestors.
I am the breath of Africa,
with the heart of my mother.
Looking with eyes into my future.
I speak the wisdom of grandmother's past.
I touch the lives of my sisters and brother.
I am one of a kind.
No one can take my shine.
I'm on a path that will carry out my dreams,
accountant, attorney, actor, writer,
I am a song waiting to be heard.
Sometimes I'm misunderstood
Yet I embrace the challenges before me.
I am Micleicia
Angel of happiness

John William Willis, Jr.

I am destined to be a leader and motivator.
I stand tall, every bit of 6ft or more.
I am proud to stand up for what is right.
I stand on the shoulders of my ancestors,
I lean on the wisdom of my father and
mother. There aren't many
young men like me. Yet I teach many
the values that I've been taught.
I can be whatever I want
But, I am destined to stand for what
Is right!
It is my duty to prepare the way for
Young men everywhere, by example.
I am John
LEADER

Johnesha Chante' Willis

I am a quiet sound, heard loudly in your ears.
I am a symbol Of Nubian beauty raging within.
Shining through.
I walk with the strength of my mother,
hard as a rock. I am wise as an Owl
but slow to speak.
All of my qualities are unique.
My eyes are the windows to my soul.
I am divinely made.
In every situation that life brings,
like a rubber band, I will bounce back.
I have the will power of a champion.

Like a target
I am for my goals.
The sky is the limit.
My dreams are as far as I can believe.
I am a fifth teen-year-old girl with a heart as pure as a baby.
But the wisdom of a young lady.
Singer of happiness

Antalicia Kierah Gray

I am the last of my siblings

I am number 4

I have the knowledge hope, peace, grace, and love left from the generation before me,

to help carry me to my destiny.

Yet, I depend on no one

I've had many things handed down to me,

strength, money, knowledge,

Yet, the choices I make in this life must be my own.

My parents have equipped me with the word of God.

My faith will see me through any situation.

I am number four,

There are three before me; they are indeed pushing me to my destiny

I am blessed to be the youngest.

Antalicia

Honor and happiness

Try believing

Try believing in the Father Son and the Holy Ghost

Believe in the saving power of Jesus Christ.

His forgiveness and grace.

His steady hand,

his tender love, and mercy.

Try believing in something real and genuine.

Something that works

Believe in Christ.

I love You

I love you because
you know me like no one else.
I love you,
You're so patient with me.
You have to be my divine husband
To understand me.
I love you,
only you can see through my stubbornness
You have stuck with me this far.
I love you for your tender heart,
Big bear hugs.
You may be sweet and sour, but you're my sour!
I love you for accepting everything about me.
I love you because I don't know what to do,
but I love you.

Where's the church

Someone just got shot.

A mother just lost her child.

Hundreds of teens are giving their children away,

while millions of fathers are disowning their children.

Our churches are not full.

Many members are sharing the word with each other,

but not reaching out to help save others.

Someone just died without Christ!

Another is paying for their death, for the rest of their life!

Yet we are still arguing, Jesus, Buddha, and Jehovah.

What will it take for us to recognize the world needs a Savior!

Not another debate, but real stories they can relate to.

A mother just walked away from her home,

she had no hope.

What will it take for us to be the voice of Christ?

What will it take for us to live right at our jobs?

As well as in our homes,

Not Just at Church!

Why must people continue to drown in pain because of our mess?

I stress we must get busy,

there are still so many who never heard of Christ,

They don't even know the price that he paid for their sins.

Let's let them know!

Let them know!

Let the choice be theirs!

A child born of a child

Who will she become?

This child born of a child,

isolated and conceived in pain.

Growing in the womb of an unwanted stranger

To be born in a world of shame.

Realizing every move, she makes is magnified and under a microscope.

For she is the product of a childhood

Pregnancy.

Looked upon as an unwanted misfit child,

who was never thrown away.

Just not nurtured with a mother's love.

How will she get strength when weakness

Surrounds her on every side?

How will she know love without a mother's love?

Who will she become?
Or what will she become?
This child born of a child!
This child is grown
Now, and strong
She grabbed ahold
of the love of
God!
His love brought
her though.
Whatever you're lacking
God's got it!

From a sister to a brother

There once,

Then gone.

Missed so

And loved dearly

Thought of

Full of joy

Mellow like a toy

Cared for just like a babe,

Now you must leave

Why, must you leave?

You whom we put so much trust in.

Felice S.C

You who, touched our hearts in a brotherly way,

You're a part of us. A part of me.

In my heart, is where your love lays.

Above all, it will stay the same.

Just as sure as your name.

There's no cure to take away the pain or make things right.

Tonight, we cry,

we tried to get God to let you stay, but he took you anyway.

My Life

One dream I have always had since I was younger,
was to publish a book or two. As far as I can remember,
I've always expressed myself through writing. I was raised
In the church, with the fear of the Lord in my heart. My
relationship with God got more personal as I got older.
I realize all good things come from God. There's no room
for anything bad in my life. I've written poems, songs, plays
, and stories. I enjoy writing, my writings are also inspirational.
I thank God all the time for using me for his glory. As a wife
And mother I'd like to leave a part of myself behind to share
with the world

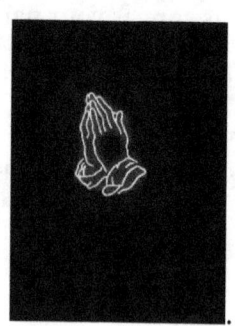

www.ingramcontent.com/pod-product-compliance
Lightning Source LLC
Chambersburg PA
CBHW050435010526
44118CB00013B/1537